Eyewitness
KNIGHT
Expert Files

Eyewitness
KNIGHT
Expert Files

DK Publishing

LONDON, NEW YORK,
MELBOURNE, MUNICH, AND DELHI

Consultant Christopher Gravett
Senior Editor Jayne Miller
Editors Kathy Fahey, Kate Scarborough, Lisa Stock
Senior Art Editor Ted Kinsey
Art Editors Susan St. Louis, Gemma Thompson
Model adapted by Chloe Luxford
Managing Editor Camilla Hallinan
Art Director Martin Wilson
Picture Research Sarah Hopper
DK Picture Library Claire Bowers, Lucy Claxton,
Rose Horridge, Emma Shepherd
Production Editor Andy Hilliard
Senior Production Controller Man Fai Lau
Jacket Designer David Ball
Eyewitness Experts concept Caroline Buckingham

First published in the United States in 2008
by DK Publishing,
375 Hudson Street, New York, New York 10014

08 09 10 11 10 9 8 7 6 5 4 3 2 1
ED626—07/08

A catalog record for this book
is available from the Library of Congress.

ISBN: 978-0-7566-4017-0

Color reproduction by Colourscan, Singapore
Printed and bound by Toppan Printing Co.
(Shenzhen) Ltd., China

Discover more at
www.dk.com

Contents

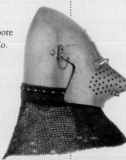

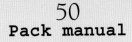

1

MEET THE EXPERTS

If you are enchanted by the age of chivalry
and inspired by lofty castles,
find out how our experts have turned
their passion for the past into a career.

EXPERT
Armorer
PROFILE

Robert "Mac" MacPherson in his workshop

Northeastern US — Philadelphia

ATLANTIC OCEAN

NAME: **ROBERT MACPHERSON**

NATIONALITY: **AMERICAN**

LIVES: **PHILADELPHIA**

Robert MacPherson trained as an entomologist, a biologist who studies insects. And although the exoskeleton—the hard outer casing—of an insect is known as its armor, there the similarity ends. Mac got into making armor by chance, while involved with a history reenactment group in college for fun. They were using protection designed for hockey and football, so he built himself some medieval-style steel armor. Soon other people asked him to make armor for them, and he found that researching and making authentic armor was more interesting than reenactment—or entomology, so he changed direction and became a professional armorer.

ON THE MAP
Mac's workshop is in Paoli, a suburb of Philadelphia known for a massacre of American soldiers by the British during the Revolutionary War, but Mac is inspired by a different era of battles. He creates replicas of medieval suits of armor, helmets, and gauntlets.

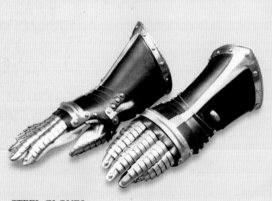

STEEL GLOVES
Beautifully crafted steel-fingered gauntlets in the style of a German pair from 1580 reveal how intricate Mac's steelwork can be. These are known as "black and whites" because the bright steel bands contrast with the black parts.

Making history from steel

FROM PLAYFIGHTING WITH A REENACTMENT GROUP
AND NEEDING SOME PROTECTION, ROBERT MACPHERSON
TAUGHT HIMSELF TO BUILD REPLICAS OF HISTORICAL
SUITS OF ARMOR. HE HAS BECOME ONE OF THE
WORLD'S FOREMOST ARMORERS.

KNIGHT IN SHINING ARMOR
Mac's armor is commissioned by collectors, reenactors, and jousters around the world—including Tobias Capwell, a curator at the Wallace Collection, London, who is jousting below on a black horse called Dietrich.

AN ARMORER'S WORKSHOP
A woodcut by Hans Burgkmair from 1515, illustrating the Austrian emperor Maximilian's autobiography, shows his view of a 16th-century armorer's workshop.

Learning the craft

When I started, there were no books on how armor was made and no instructions to follow, so I had to practically reinvent the craft, to discover what real armor looked like and try to figure out how it was made. That is what I have been doing ever since. Sadly, the tradition of armorers passing on their skills to apprentices died out in the 17th and early 18th centuries, but there are still all manner of smiths, and their tools and techniques survive. I read everything I could on coppersmithing and blacksmithing. I also researched silversmithing to see how punch-bowls and goblets were made. Then I adapted the processes to make steel armor.

The right tools for the job

You can't just go to the store and buy armorer's tools. I use some hammers and anvils meant for blacksmiths who shoe horses or make gates and hinges. Many of my tools are antiques, bought at markets. Others started out as big chunks of rail track that I formed into specific useful shapes. Armorers also adapt modern tools—I have some

that were designed for car repairs. I can't say my workshop has the same tools as one in the Middle Ages, because we just don't know. There are a handful of old pictures of medieval armorers at work, but very few of them really show tools. One famous picture by Hans Burgkmair has tools spread out—although I don't have exactly the same ones, my workbench is usually at least that cluttered.

Picturing the past

Not much armor has survived. Most of what you see in museums is from the last days of armor. If you want to see what early armor looked like, you have to look at paintings, drawings, and statues. Even then, although medieval illustrations may be based on real armor, it might not be the right armor for the time. And many of the interesting details are around the back of the body, which you almost never see in pictures. Most of my customers come with an idea of what armor they want. They know

IDEAS IN STONE
This effigy of the Duke of Somerset, who died in 1444, was the main reference for Tobias Capwell's suit.

Many important details are at the back

KNIGHT IN ARMOR
Tobias Capwell came to Mac with the idea for an English medieval suit of armor that he could wear while jousting. Tobias had spent four years researching the suit—it took Mac two years to build.

what time period and what country they want it to be from—or what famous battle the armor would have been used in. Some have a firm but historically bogus idea, so I have to try to steer them a little. I don't do fantasy armor. Most of my work is based on armor that did exist or that I am reasonably sure could have existed.

Man with a mission

Tobias Capwell, a Canadian curator, spent four years studying English 15th-century armor. Little was known about it before his work, because hardly any survived. Tobias visited over 600 churches and took thousands of pictures of effigies of knights. These are life-sized sculptures of deceased knights lying on their funeral beds. They show suits of armor in detail, right down to the rivets and decoration. My task was to build armor for Tobias in the style of an English knight from 1450, a feat that had not been accomplished in 550 years.

"There were no instructions to follow, so I had to practically reinvent the craft ... to try to figure out how armor was made. That is what I have been doing ever since."

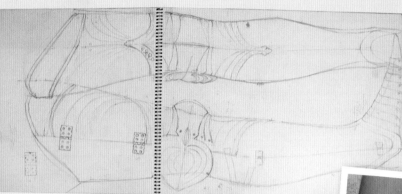

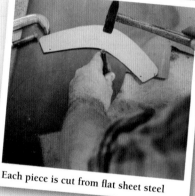

Each piece is cut from flat sheet steel

Work in progress

Tobias's armor took about two years to build, partly because he was working as curator of arms and armor for Glasgow Museums in Scotland (and later at The Wallace Collection in London) a long way from my workshop. He came to the US for initial measurements and then only for occasional fittings. As with all suits and pieces of armor, I started by taking detailed measurements. I always make a series of tracings around the person and put the measurements on these. They stand against a wall with a piece of paper behind them and I do one tracing from the front and one from the side. I take two chest measurements—one with their arms by their side, then they breathe in and raise their arms so the chest swells. For the waist, I'll say, "Just stand comfortably. Now pull your stomach in as if trying to look good at the beach. Now let your stomach stick out like you're Homer Simpson." I use these measurements to work out how far I can pull the armor in and keep it comfortable. For a slim guy the figures won't differ very much, but for a big man it could differ by 6–8 inches (15–17 cm)!

Rebuilding history

Next, I make the sketches, first small scale, then full size. I transfer all the body tracings to a notebook, one limb at a time, and draw the armor over these outlines, including the decorative details. Once I know what the armor is going to look like, I use the drawings to make up cardboard templates of each

HAMMERING AWAY
Some hammer work is done on cold metal, some needs heat. Mac uses an oxyacetylene torch (a gas torch that produces a high temperature) to heat the pieces for hot work.

"Like me, most armorers are making armor with modern methods, not medieval ones"

work is best done over a steel ball—mine is 9 inches (22 cm) across. Medieval armorers would not have been able to get nicely rolled flat sheet metal like I use. They were starting with a smaller, thicker piece, so had a different way of making their armor. Unfortunately, we don't know what that method was. Like me, most armorers are making armor with modern methods, not medieval ones.

piece. I take cardboard and start hacking it away until I have a good starting shape for a breastplate and all the rest of the pieces. Then I transfer these shapes to flat sheet steel. I trace around each piece and cut it out with an electric reciprocating saw—medieval armorers probably used chisels and shears. After that, I hammer each piece into shape. Every square inch of the piece must be hammered. Real armor has no flat spots and I don't let mine have any either!

Raising armor

Helmets, breastplates, and pieces with a lot of depth are made with a technique called "raising." You start in the middle of the piece and each hammer blow in the center sends a sort of wave of metal about ¾ in (2 cm) high out and toward the edge. One "pass," or hammering session, might take an hour, and a helmet may have a dozen or so passes before it is deep enough. This is hard work, and you sweat hard and have to be careful not to injure yourself. Raising is a technique I learned from silversmiths and coppersmiths. They use a tool called a T-stake—a narrow metal anvil (block) with a slightly rounded top. I find that for helmets and breastplates this

LIFELIKE LEGS
Plaster leg casts allow Mac to work on the greaves (lower leg pieces) at length without the customer having to stand around.

A cast of thousands

It would be perfect if each customer could stay in the shop while I make their armor, but they have other things to do. I can generally make do with measurements and tracings, but not for the lower legs—as these are the most difficult parts of the harness (armor) to make because of the delicate curves. So I make plaster replicas of each customer's legs, from their toes to their knees. Then, when I am working on the sabatons (foot armor) or greaves (shin armor), I can continually check the armor against the plaster replicas. In many ways this is better, because the plaster replicas never complain they are bored, or that the metal is too hot, too cold, or too wet.

A FITTING SESSION
Once the individual pieces are beaten into shape, they have to be fitted to one another—here the poleyn (the knee piece) is put together with the cuisse (thigh protection).

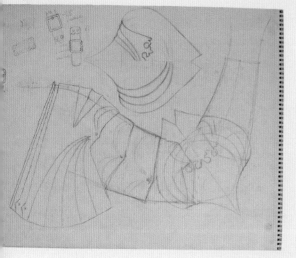

MOVEABLE JOINTS
Overlapping pieces of steel (lames) allow the arm harness to flex at the shoulder and elbow as the arm moves.

Piecing it together
Once the shape has been hammered to a smooth finish, I assemble all the plates temporarily with nuts and bolts. This gives me a chance to fine-tune how the pieces fit and work together. Some of my customers ask for modifications—they say, "Can you engineer in more knee motion?" Yes I could, but I won't because it won't look right! Besides, if you make a piece of armor flex more, it will have bigger gaps and will be less protective. You should have enough motion to lift your foot and put it in the stirrup of your horse; to bend over enough to pick up your sword if you drop it; and to kneel long enough to be knighted; but not to do yoga!

Treating the armor
When I'm satisfied that everything is working perfectly, I heat the pieces in a kiln until they are red hot, then quench (cool) them in water. This makes them very hard—too hard. To keep them from being brittle, I heat each piece again, this time to a lower temperature so that the metal relaxes. When this heat treatment is finished, the pieces are like springs— hard, but able to move and return to their original shape without

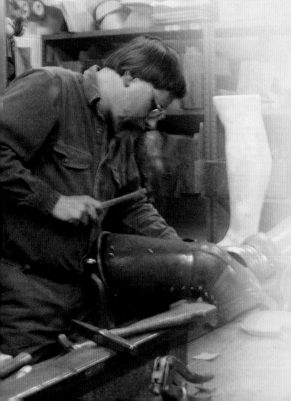

MECHANICAL KNEE
Mac holds the joints together temporarily with nuts and bolts so he can make the fine adjustments that let the joint bend smoothly.

A MODEL KNIGHT
This 15th-century German suit of armor is another of Mac's projects. It is arranged on an adjustable life-sized wooden stand that Mac made, to give an idea of what it will look like on its owner.

"At this point, the armor is dented from the hammer, black from the furnace, and rusty—it looks awful!"

breaking. At this point, the armor is dented from the hammer, black from the furnace, and rusty. It looks awful! I grind out the hammer marks until the surfaces are perfectly smooth. Then I sand off the grinding marks, then polish off the sanding marks to make the surface smooth and shiny. This process can take almost half the entire production time.

Knight in shining armor
Some armor is bright and silver-colored. Tobias wanted his to be black. A black oxide finish was applied by a specialized company that works on gun parts and machinery—they had never worked on armor before! When I took the pieces of the suit to them, I had finished everything except riveting them together—each piece was like silver mirror. When I picked them up, they were black mirrors. Tobias's suit was ready to be tested in the field of battle. He wanted to wear it in a tournament in Holland, so I took it over to him and helped to dress him. It is essential to have help—and to have the right undergarment, an arming doublet. This is a kind of close-fitting jacket, made of strong fabric because the armor will be tied onto it. Each piece is strapped on in turn. When the knight is nearly ready to fight, on goes the helmet and finally the gauntlets. After a few tweaks, Tobias was ready to joust. It was a thrilling moment for the knight—and for me, the armorer.

IT FITS!
Tobias has worn his suit in many jousting events, including this tournament at Lulworth Castle, Dorset, UK.

Types of expert

Historians, who study particular eras or subjects from the past, are vital to our understanding of medieval times, but many other experts also help to give us an insight into what life in medieval times was really like. Museums, reenacting centers, and documentary makers, among others, work to bring the past to life for a wide audience.

CONSERVATOR

Conservators play an important role in preserving medieval artifacts for future generations to study and enjoy. Their work ranges from day-to-day care of museum collections to the repair and restoration of recently discovered finds. Sometimes conservators reconstruct badly damaged pieces and supply elements that are missing, and so they need to have an extensive knowledge of the subjects on which they work. They also need a good overall understanding of the historical period from which their objects come, along with the scientific knowledge of techniques that will preserve valuable pieces.

PRESERVING THE PAST
At London's Wallace Collection, a conservator carefully removes tarnish from a 16th-century shaffron—a horse's head piece. She wears gloves to prevent the oil from her skin form getting on the metal, as this can contribute to erosion.

REPLICA MAKER

When weapons and armor appear in reenactments, documentaries, and films, it is not usually actual artifacts that you see, since these might be damaged; instead, replicas are made to look the part. Replica makers study authentic pieces and then recreate them to mimic the original as closely as possible. Sometimes they use traditional methods, but many large workshops have modern equipment to make replicas in the quantities required. Some replicas are so well made that it takes an expert to tell the difference between the replica and the real thing. Armor and replica weapons are also made for museums and private collectors.

CREATING A SWORD
A replica maker examines the blade of a sword he is making for a film. The hilt, or handle, will only be added once the blade is finished.

CURATOR

A curator, or keeper, looks after the artifacts in a collection and acquires new pieces to add to it. These precious items are cataloged and displayed. They also organize exhibitions, as well as the loan of items to other museums. Curators have in-depth knowledge of the artifacts they look after and are familiar with the methods used to conserve them. They often help researchers who visit museums to enhance their studies. Curators also give lectures and may act as consultants for film and television companies who want to make historically accurate films.

ARMOR ON DISPLAY
Deciding the best way to display an artifact to impress the visitors is an important part of a curator's job. Here a suit of armor is posed as though a knight is wearing it, to give an idea of the warrior's size and stature.

ART HISTORIAN

An art historian has spent many years studying the development of art in a certain historical period. While most people think of art history as the study of paintings, art historians may be experts in many other kinds of art, such as painting, tapestry, woodwork, or metalwork. Much can be learned about a society from its art. Some illuminations in medieval manuscripts show us the way that medieval people dressed, fought, and grew crops.

CAREFUL CLEANING
Decorative wooden panels in Chastleton House, Oxfordshire, are cleaned using a soft-bristled brush. Overcleaning would destroy the patina (aged finish).

REENACTOR

The job of the reenactor is to imitate as realistically as possible the occupations of people who lived in a particular historial period. Good reenactors can make history come to life for the audience watching them and give them a better understanding of how people lived. Some of the most popular medieval reenactments are displays of fighting or jousting.

SWORDPLAY
Two reenactors wearing replica armor from the 13th century practice their swordfighting for a mock battle.

MASTER CRAFTSMAN

When a historical building needs restoration and repair, master craftsmen and women carry out the work. They are experts in traditional methods of carpentry and construction and will try to match surviving materials as closely as possible. Although traditional methods may take longer than modern ones, the result will be more historically accurate. Traditional craftsmen also work with artifacts and replicas.

TRADITIONAL WOODWORK
A bowyer creates an authentic longbow from wood following traditional craft techniques.

DOCUMENTARY MAKER

Documentary makers are often filmmakers with an interest in a particular subject, such as archeology. Sometimes they have an opinion about a subject that they want to show, but often they just want to give an overview of a subject to get people interested in it. Documentaries can be great learning tools and are popular with television audiences, too.

TIME TEAM IN ACTION
British TV host Tony Robinson and the Time Team (Channel 4) crew work on cleaning artifacts found during a dig while the camera rolls.

MEDIEVAL ARCHEOLOGIST

Archeologists who specialize in the medieval period need a thorough understanding of the period and its artifacts as well as technical knowledge about archeological methods in general. Archeologists may supervise trained volunteers. Work on a dig proceeds slowly and painstakingly, so that nothing of importance is missed.

EXCAVATING A SITE
Locations near castles are often excavated for medieval artifacts because people lived close to castles for protection.

Tools and techniques

WHEN RESTORING OR RECREATING ARMOR AND WEAPONS or other artifacts from previous centuries, specialists use many tools and techniques that are similar to those used in the Middle Ages. Some are modern versions of old equipment, such as power-driven drills, but some are completely new. Workers today benefit from safety gear, such as protective eyewear and heat-proof gloves that their medieval counterparts never had, making the job much less dangerous.

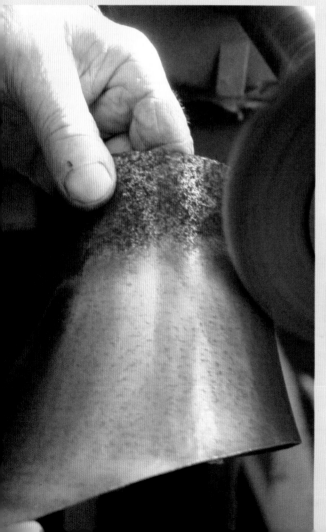

RESTORATION

Experts take great care to restore or re-create pieces of armor as accurately as possible. Often armor pieces need new internal leathers (that fastened the pieces together) since the originals have decayed. Then the armor pieces can be put together as they once would have appeared. Rivets might need to be replaced and sometimes holes in the plates caused by rust or damage are carefully repaired with new metal. Sometimes missing pieces from a suit of armor are researched and copied, so that the suit can be rebuilt as a complete armor.

RUST REMOVAL
Rust is removed from a piece of armor using a polishing wheel. It gives the armor the same finish it would have had when new.

HAMMERS
A rounded type of metalworking hammer, called a ball peen hammer, is used to shape metal and fasten rivets.

BUILDING REPAIR

Uncovering and restoring ancient buildings requires a knowledge of old building techniques, and it is important for restorers to use materials that match the originals as closely as possible. Although restorers cannot always use traditional tools for larger tasks due to the amount of time and money it would take, they may finish a job using traditional methods so that the outer appearance of the building remains authentic.

ARCHEOLOGISTS TOOLS

Small picks, hand trowels, and brushes are the main tools archeologists use to uncover treasures from the past. At a dig, an archeologist always scrapes the dirt away to retrieve an artifact—they never dig it out, because that could damage it.

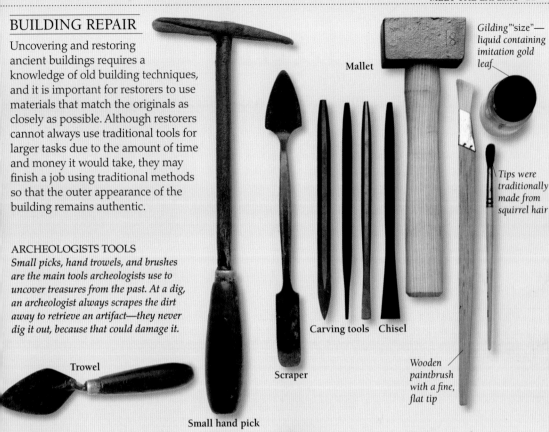

Gilding "size"—liquid containing imitation gold leaf

Mallet

Tips were traditionally made from squirrel hair

Trowel

Carving tools   Chisel

Scraper

Wooden paintbrush with a fine, flat tip

Small hand pick

Work gloves

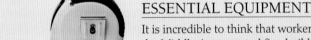

Tape measure

DUST AND POLISH

Apart from repairing and restoring artifacts, much of an expert's work involves preserving the pieces for future generations. Once repaired, metals must be rubbed with a wax (called microcrystalline wax) to keep off dust and moisture.

Polish and cloth

ESSENTIAL EQUIPMENT

It is incredible to think that workers in the Middle Ages created fine buildings and craftwork with the limited tools they had available. Modern restorers have access to computers to make calculations or use laser measurers where the original craftsmen would have used yardsticks or other less precise ways of measuring. Similarly, restorers might use wood that has been treated with preservatives to prevent rotting, so that repairs will be longer lasting. Tools and techniques such as these do not affect the appearance of a building, but they ensure that it will still be standing for many years to come.

Hall of fame

THE EARLIEST MEDIEVAL EXPERTS were scholars and knights who wrote about their own pursuits and collections. Their writings have inspired historians and curators over the centuries, who in turn have added to our knowledge of knights and life in the Middle Ages.

CLAUDE BLAIR
1922 TO PRESENT
JOB: Expert on armor & silver
COUNTRY: UK

One of the world's leading experts on arms and armor, Blair has written many books and articles on historic metalwork and arms. His *Arms and Armor* is considered a definitive work on the subject. Blair also put together a famed two-volume work on the British crown jewels. He was Keeper of the Department of Metalwork at the Victoria & Albert Museum in London from 1972 until 1982, and now sits on various arts boards.

WENDELIN BOEHEIM
1832-1900
JOB: Expert on arms and armor
COUNTRY: Austria

The famous Austrian scholar Wendelin Boeheim was a university professor in Vienna and Director of the Imperial Collection of Armor, Austria. His research on European armor was considered important for its account of 15th- and 16th-century armorers, whose designs had not been studied before. He was particularly interested in the sabaton—armor for the feet.

R. ALLEN BROWN
1924-1989
JOB: Professor of history
COUNTRY: UK

Allen Brown was a professor of medieval history at King's College, London, and an international expert on castles. He wrote many books, such as *The Origins of English Feudalism*, as well as *English Castles*, which is prized by other experts.

CHARLES BUTTIN
1856-1931
JOB: Armor expert & collector
COUNTRY: France

Charles Buttin wrote more than 100 studies of European and Oriental arms and armor and was one of the foremost authorities on

armor of his day. He built up his own huge collection of arms and armor, which has now been sold.

Charles Buttin at work in his study

SIR GEOFFROI DE CHARNY
1300-1356
JOB: Medieval knight
COUNTRY: France

Geoffroi de Charny was a medieval knight who managed to write several books on chivalry during his illustrious military career. The most famous of these is probably his *Book of Chivalry*, written around 1350, which puts strong emphasis on skill with arms. With a reputation for being pious and honorable as well as brave, de Charny was a model knight, and served as the standard bearer for France in the Hundred Years War.

Detail from de Charny's journal

ROBERT COLTMAN CLEPHAN
1839-1922
JOB: Expert on arms and Egypt
COUNTRY: UK

The English scholar and collector Robert Coltman Clephan was born in Gateshead and served as a captain in the Durham Rifle Corps. He became an expert on medieval arms with a good collection of his own, and wrote works on medieval siege engines and tournaments. A scholar of diverse interests, he was also an expert on firearms, and later developed an interest in Egypt, traveling there for research.

BARON CHARLES A. DE COSSON
1846-1929
JOB: Expert on arms and armor
COUNTRY: UK

The descendant of an aristocratic French family that came to England to escape the French Revolution, Baron de Cosson became interested in armor when he bought a toy suit of armor as a boy. He began collecting armor seriously in 1872, eventually becoming the foremost authority on European armor of his day.

ANNE CURRY
1954 TO PRESENT
JOB: Professor of history
COUNTRY: UK

Currently Professor of History at the University of Southampton and president of the Historical Association, Anne Curry is a world expert on the Battle of Agincourt. Her book *Agincourt: A New History* argues that the English were not as greatly outnumbered in this defining battle as has been believed for the last six centuries. She has also conducted research into medieval women and warfare and created a database of soldiers who fought in the Hundred Years War (from 1337 to 1453) that people can search for ancestors.

BASHFORD DEAN
1867-1928
JOB: Armor curator, zoologist
COUNTRY: US

The American scholar Bashford Dean was an expert in zoology as well as medieval armor and is the only person to have held posts simultaneously at the American Museum of Natural History and the Metropolitan Museum of Art in New York. He began collecting arms at the age of ten, and later advised the US military on designs for a new helmet during World War I.

Bashford Dean

VISCOUNT DILLON
1844-1932
JOB: Expert on arms and armor
COUNTRY: UK

Harold Arthur Lee-Dillon, 17th Viscount of Costello-Gallen, served in the Rifle Brigade as a young man and was initially interested only in modern weaponry. Later he became fascinated by medieval arms and armor as well and became a leading expert in the field, serving as the Curator of Armories at the Tower of London. He often wrote scholarly pieces under the pseudonym "Armadillo." Although curator of one of the largest collections of armor in the world, Viscount Dillon owned only two pieces of armor himself.

KING DUARTE OF PORTUGAL
1391-1438
JOB: Medieval king
COUNTRY: Portugal

Often called "the Philosopher" or "the Eloquent," King Duarte of Portugal was a medieval ruler who wrote poems and books while governing his country. He is most famous for writing *The Art of Good Horsemanship*, a 15th-century treatise on how to ride using various types of saddle and how to joust. The book is divided into three parts, but the final section remains unfinished because the king died of the plague before he was able to complete it.

King Duarte statue, Viseu, Portugal

VERONICA FIORATO
1969 TO PRESENT
JOB: Archeologist
COUNTRY: UK/ITALY

Veronica Fiorato instigated research on mass graves found during an excavation of the Towtown Battlefield in Yorkshire, UK, the site of one of the bloodiest battles of the Wars of the Roses in 1461. It was the first modern investigation of a mass grave from a medieval European battlefield and made use of forensic science (investigative) techniques. Research on the skeletons there revealed much about medieval warfare. She also co-wrote a book on the excavations called *Blood Red Roses*. Veronica, who says visits to castles and abbeys as a child fired her interest in the past, now works for English Heritage, which helps to protect historic buildings and sites.

CLAUDE GAIER
1938 TO PRESENT
JOB: Firearms curator
COUNTRY: Belgium

Claude Gaier's main field of interest is early firearms, although he is also an expert on medieval arms and warfare in general. Gaier is particularly knowledgeable about the firearms that were produced in the area around the Belgian city of Liège, which was an early center of firearms manufacture. He is Curator of the Liège Firearms Museum—the second largest arms museum in Europe—where he has expanded its collections. The museum owns over 13,000 arms-related objects dating back to the 14th century when Liège began to produce weapons.

JOHN HEWITT
1807–1878
JOB: Scholar of arms and armor
COUNTRY: UK

Originally destined for a musical career, John Hewitt was also a talented organist and spoke several languages as well as being an arms expert. He joined the staff of the War Office as a young man and eventually took on responsibility for the national collection of arms at the Tower of London. During his career there he wrote the very first guide to the Tower and its armory. It was so good that it set a new standard in arms scholarship. Many English, German, and French writers relied on Hewitt's painstaking research.

Tower of London

TERRY JONES
1942 TO PRESENT
JOB: Popular historian
COUNTRY: Wales

After studying English at Oxford, Terry Jones became a successful actor and comedy writer as part of the Monty Python troupe and also directed several films. He has written books for children and has presented television shows on ancient and medieval history in which he aims to make history fun. He also wrote a study of the knight in Chaucer's *Canterbury Tales*,

Terry Jones in *Medieval Lives*

portraying the knight as a typical medieval mercenary—someone who fought for money.

MAURICE KEEN
1933 TO PRESENT
JOB: Medieval historian
COUNTRY: UK

Now an honorary Professor, Maurice Keen lectured in medieval history at Oxford from 1961 until he retired in 2000. An expert on medieval warfare, his books include *The Laws of War in the Late Middle Ages* and *Medieval Warfare: A History*. He is also interested in all aspects of chivalry across Europe. His book *Chivalry* was awarded the Wolfson History Prize in 1984.

CARL OTTO VON KIENBUSCH
1884–1972
JOB: Collector of armor
COUNTRY: US

Born in New York in 1884, the American arms and armor expert Karl Otto Kretzschmar von Kienbusch had one of the world's largest collections of medieval European armor. He graduated from Princeton in 1906, and began collecting arms around 1914. Von Kienbusch was able to combine a successful business career with his passion for collecting. He left his collection to the Philadelphia Museum of Art in Pennyslvania.

SIR GUY FRANCIS LAKING
1875-1919

JOB: Arms scholar and collector

COUNTRY: UK

As the son of a doctor who treated the royal household, Sir Guy Laking had many aristocratic connections. Although interested in armor as a boy, he originally intended to become an architect. He met the arms collector Baron de Cosson in 1891. By 1902 Laking was Keeper of the King's Armory at Windsor, and later was Inspector at the Wallace Collection.

RAIMON LULL
C.1235-1315

JOB: Knight, mystic, missionary

COUNTRY: Spain

Raimon Lull, also sometimes called Raymond Lully, came from the Catalan region of Spain and was a mystic and missionary as well as a knight. A deeply religious man, his

A page from *The Order of Chivalry*

book *The Order of Chivalry* was modeled on the monastic rule of St. Benedict. Lull was killed on a trip to Messina, where he was trying to win converts to Christianity.

SAMUEL RUSH MEYRICK
1783-1848

JOB: Lawyer, scholar, writer

COUNTRY: UK

Samuel Rush Meyrick

Generally considered to be the founder of arms studies in the UK, Samuel Rush Meyrick was interested in antiquities of all kinds from an early age. He was a practicing lawyer as well as an arms collector, and also did extensive research on Welsh antiquities. His famous three-volume study on the development of arms, published in 1824, was the first systematic exploration of the subject, and illustrated with his own paintings.

ALEXANDER V. B. NORMAN
1930-1998

JOB: Keeper of arms and armor

COUNTRY: UK

Nick Norman, as he was known, was born in Delhi in India but raised in Scotland. He was a renowned expert on arms and on small swords and rapiers in particular. He also studied monumental effigies (the sculptures that often appear on medieval tombs). Over the course of his long career, he first became Keeper at the Wallace Collection and was later Master of the

Armories at the Tower of London. While there, he organized a fund-raising appeal for the Royal Armories to buy a private 17th-century armory, now displayed at Leeds. Norman wrote many books on knightly subjects, including *English Weapons and Warfare*.

SIR CHARLES OMAN
1860-1946

JOB: Military historian

COUNTRY: UK

Sir Charles Oman was born in India, but he later returned to England, and studied at Oxford. Oman is seen as one of England's greatest military historians. He used medieval accounts of battles to reconstruct the scenes in his books and bring them to life. His books, written with verve and flair, became the definitive works on medieval warfare of their day.

DR. YOSHIHIKO SASAMA
1916-2005

JOB: Scholar of arms and armor

COUNTRY: Japan

As the leading authority on Japanese arms and armor, Dr. Yoshihiko Sasama wrote over 50 books on the subject; many of these have become the standard reference books to use. He was an expert on *katchu-shi*, or Japanese armorers, as well as on Samurai arms.

Japanese arms and armor

2

ACTIVITIES

Are you ready for knight school? Find out how much you know and hone your skills with our challenging activities.

Which expert are you?

Inspired by the exciting lives of the knight and castle experts you have read about, you are set on working in the field, but which area? Are you most suited to research, excavation, restoration, or maybe enacting? Try our fun flowchart and find out!

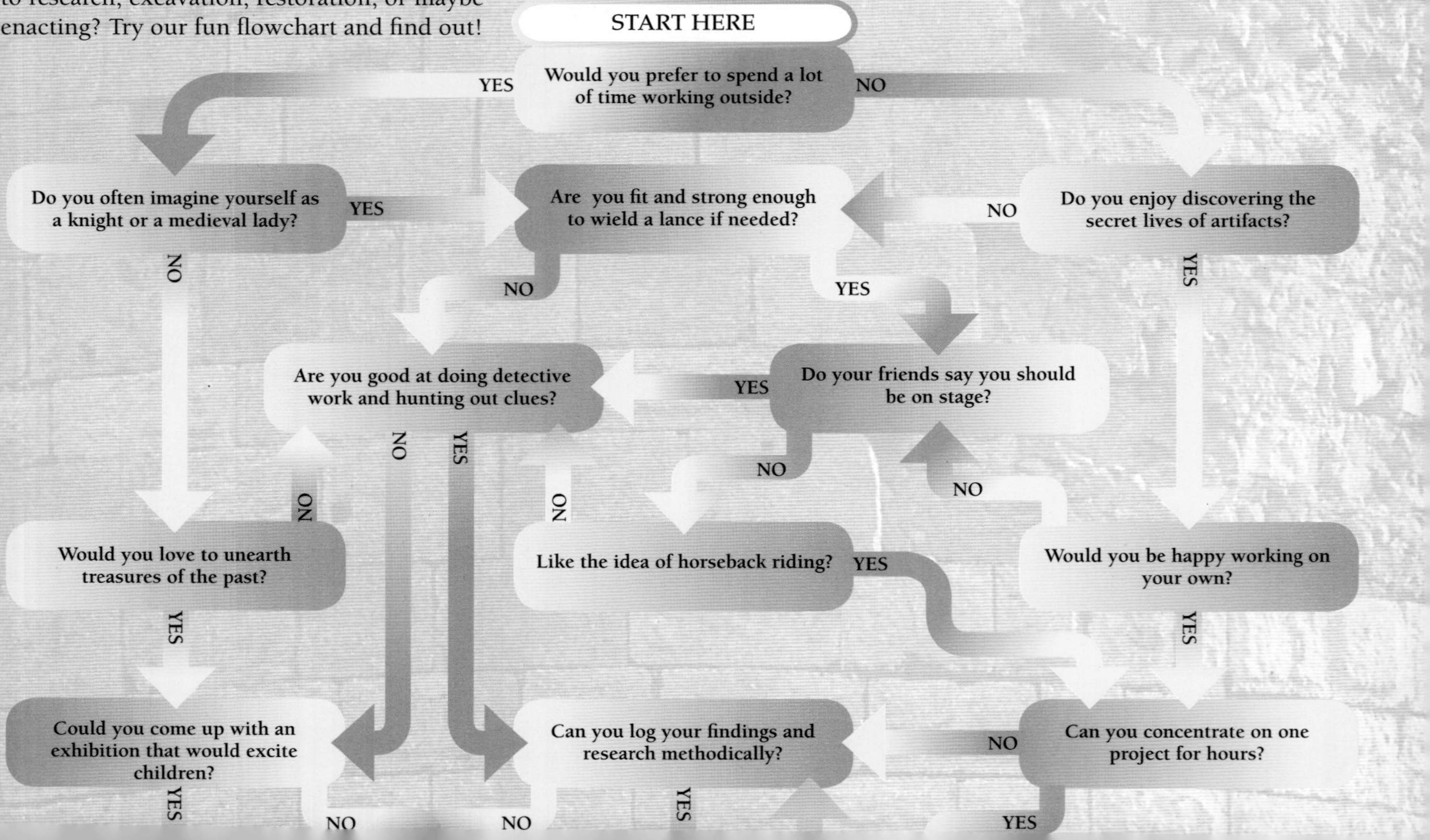

START HERE

Would you prefer to spend a lot of time working outside?

Do you enjoy discovering the secret lives of artifacts?

YES

NO

NO

Do you often imagine yourself as a knight or a medieval lady?

YES

Are you fit and strong enough to wield a lance if needed?

YES

NO

Would you be happy working on your own?

YES

Can you concentrate on one project for hours?

NO

YES

Do your friends say you should be on stage?

YES

NO

Are you good at doing detective work and hunting out clues?

YES

NO

Like the idea of horseback riding?

YES

ON

Can you log your findings and research methodically?

YES

NO

Would you love to unearth treasures of the past?

ON

YES

Could you come up with an exhibition that would excite children?

YES

NO

Do you prefer vivid dramatic films to factually correct documentaries?

NO ──→ Are you a whizz with polish and a duster?

YES ──→ Do you look at castle ruins and wonder what they looked like in their glory?

ON

Do you enjoy performing or talking in front of your class?

YES ──→ Are you a bit of a bookworm?

NO

YES / NO

Could you spend hours, days even, meticulously sifting through dirt?

Do you love dressing up in authentic costumes?

NO

YES

HISTORIAN

You love everything about the medieval world, and long to know more. You can spend hours finding out about the lives of the people who lived in the era and the artists behind the works of art.

REENACTOR

Just reading about knights isn't enough, you long to be one. Joining an authentic reenactment group would help you put your research into practice, and inspire an audience.

ARCHEOLOGIST

You can't wait to get your hands dirty in your quest to uncover secrets lost for centuries under earth or rubble. You are organised and work well as part of a team.

CURATOR

Being around suits of armor and other artifacts would be a thrill. You'd enjoy hunting out the stories behind them and devising an appealing display to show them off.

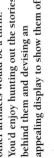

A knight's world

LEVEL 1

The first knights fought for their lords and protected his peasants in ninth-century Europe. This way of life lasted until the 16th century. Major events took place during this time. Can you order the events below, numbering them 1–6, and then add their dates?

HOW LONG
DID IT TAKE YOU?

☐ 10 mins:
Expert

☐ 15 mins:
Knowledgable

☐ 20 mins:
Beginner

There's a section full of dates in your *Eyewitness Knight* to help you.

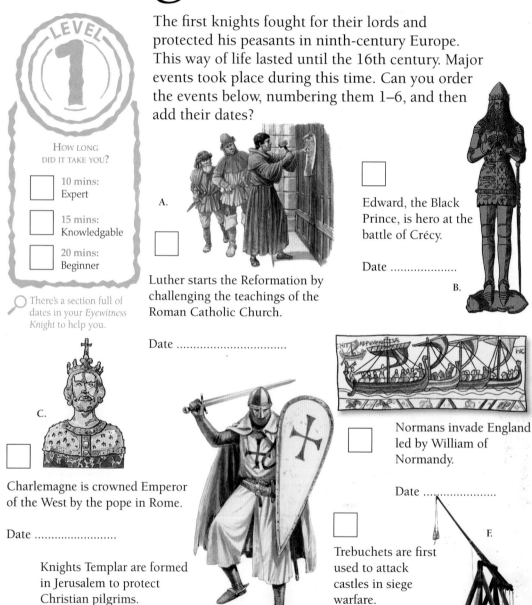

A.

☐ Luther starts the Reformation by challenging the teachings of the Roman Catholic Church.

Date ....

☐ Edward, the Black Prince, is hero at the battle of Crécy.

Date ....

B.

C.

☐ Charlemagne is crowned Emperor of the West by the pope in Rome.

Date ....

Knights Templar are formed in Jerusalem to protect Christian pilgrims.

Date ....

E.

☐ Normans invade England led by William of Normandy.

Date ....

☐ Trebuchets are first used to attack castles in siege warfare.

F.

Date ....

Spot the castle

To defend themselves and their people, wealthy landowners built huge, strong castles during the Middle Ages. These castles can be found all over Europe. Can you name each of these castles and say which country it is in?

🔍 Use your Profile Cards to help you capture the castles.

A. ....

....

B. ....   C. ....

....

D. ....

....

E. ....   F. ....

....

Know your armor

By the 15th century, knights were wearing full suits of armor. Each piece was designed to protect a different part of the body.

Test your expertise by labeling the different parts of this suit of armor.

Knights in shining armor will come to your rescue in *Eyewitness Knight*.

1 ....
2 ....
3 ....
4 ....
5 ....
6 ....

Get ahead with helmets

These six helmets appear in *Eyewitness Knight*. Where were they made and in which century?

A.

Where ....

Century ....

B.

Where ....

Century ....

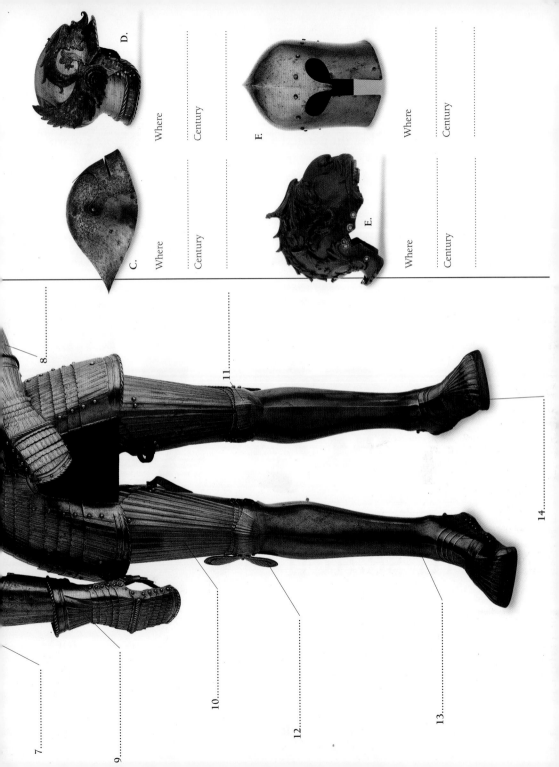

C.

Where ....

Century ....

D.

Where ....

Century ....

E.

Where ....

Century ....

F.

Where ....

Century ....

7 ....

8 ....

9 ....

10 ....

11 ....

12 ....

13 ....

14 ....

Dressing a knight

LEVEL 2

Putting on a suit of armor was so complicated that a knight needed a squire to help him. Can you work out the order in which a knight dons his armor and name the piece the squire is fitting?

How long
DID IT TAKE YOU?

☐ 10 mins:
Expert

☐ 15 mins:
Knowledgable

☐ 20 mins:
Beginner

🔍 *Eyewitness Knight*
has a step-by-step
guide on how to
dress to impress.

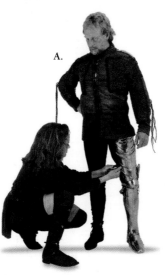

A.

B.

☐ ....

☐ ....

Sword search

Knights used a range of weapons for fighting. Can you match the names below with the weapons shown here?

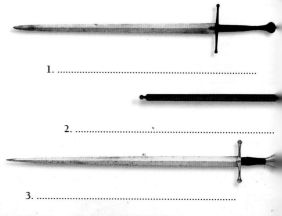

1. ....

2. ....

3. ....

ARMOR	
Two-hand sword	Dagger
Sword with	Poleax
copper-gilt guard	Mace

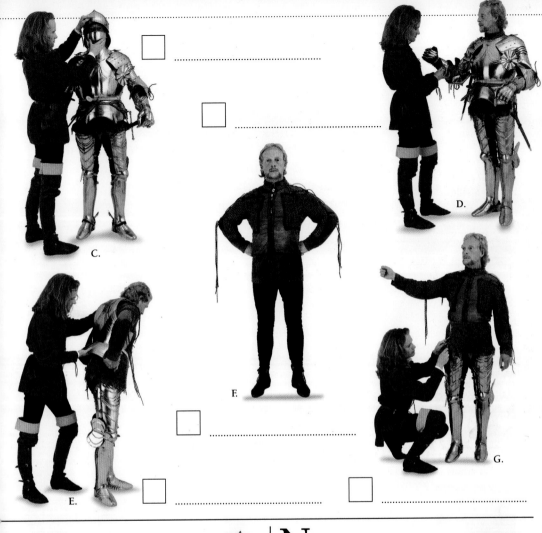

C.

D.

F.

E.

G.

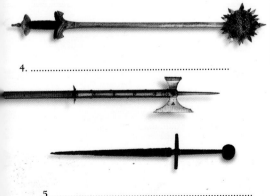

4. ....

5. ....

Name this item

Who and what is it for?

Name

....

Use

....

Heraldry

The practice of decorating shields became standard in the 12th century to help identify different knights during tournaments. Here's your chance to design your own coat-of-arms. You could either use traditional images and colors or make up your own to reflect your interests.

How long
DID IT TAKE YOU?

☐ 10 mins:
Expert

☐ 15 mins:
Knowledgable

☐ 20 mins:
Beginner

You'll find *Eyewitness Knight* has the key to decipher heraldic terms.

Lozengy argent and gules

Azure, a fleur-de-lys or

Azure and gules, fleur-de-lys and lions or

Name

....

Showy shields

If you need to know your ors from your argents try *Eyewitness Knight*.

Do you know the correct heraldic terms to name the colors and the symbols on each of the shields below?

A.

Color of background

....

Object and color

....

B.

Color of background

....

Object and color

....

C.

Color of background

....

Object and color

....

D.

Color of background

....

Object and color

....

E.

Color of background

....

Object and color

....

F.

Color of background

....

Object and color

....

Joust a minute

Can you label the different parts of a jousting knight and his horse?

You'll need to hunt around *Eyewitness Knight* to find the name for the horse's covering.

1...

2...

3...

4.....................................

5...

6.......................................

7...

Castle as kingdom

Castles were built to house a large number of people, keep them safe, and feed them. Draw a line to the right part of the castle, choosing from the list below.

CASTLE LABELS

1. Lord's apartment
2. Kitchen garden
3. Drawbridge
4. Battlement
5. Moat
6. Mural tower
7. Store rooms
8. Great Hall
9. Slit window
10. Gatehouse

....

....

....

....

Shape sorter

Can you identify the motte and bailey, keep, and concentric castles?

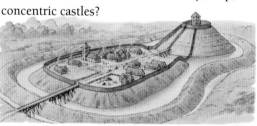

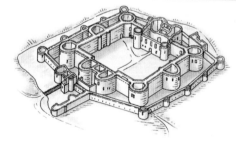

3. ....

1. ....

2. ....

Castle under siege

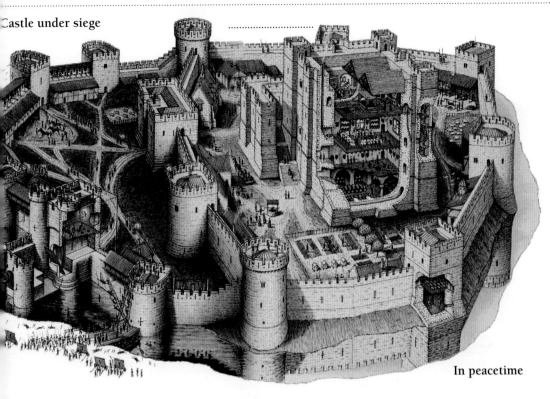

....

In peacetime

....

Defense and attack

Unscramble these words to reveal siege weapons and defenses. Are they used for attack or defense?

Word		Attack or defense
urbchette	....	....
gintabert arm	....	....
serubream	....	....
corbsows	....	....
cpsrtullio	....	....

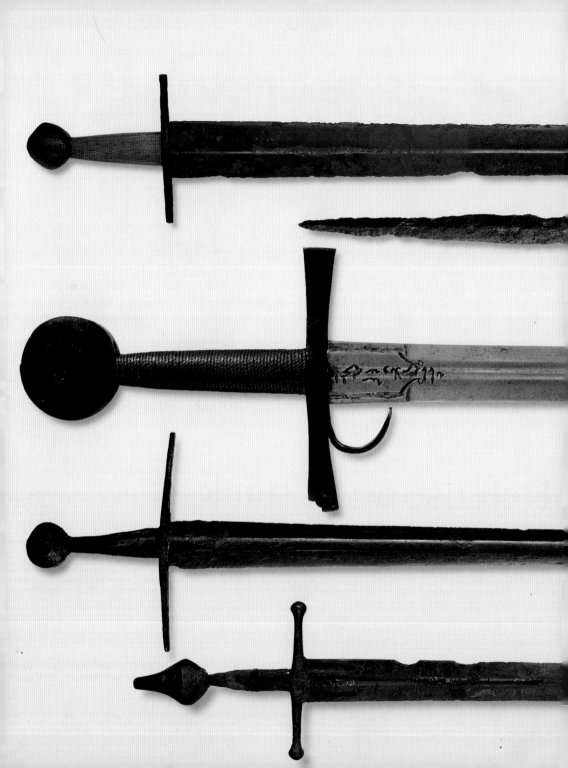

3

EXPERTS' LOG

It's time to get organized and start your own research. Get some tips on the tools that every budding expert needs. Your path to a knighthood starts here!

At the museum

Tools
- Pen and pencil
- Notebook
- Camera

• Visit an armory museum to get a closer look at medieval weapons and suits of armor and find out how knights lived, dressed, and fought. Some museums have workshops where you can learn more about the displays, and see for yourself what armor felt like!

• Step back in time by visiting a reconstructed medieval town, such as the Danish Medieval Center in Copenhagen, Denmark, where you can watch knights joust, shoot arrows from a longbow, and see people strolling by wearing the fashions of the Middle Ages.

• Galleries around the world display art and architecture from medieval Europe. You could find fascinating paintings and beautiful stained-glass windows, as well as artifacts such as manuscripts, enamels, and tapestries.

• Make notes here from the information cards that accompany your favorite exhibits. Try to find out as much as you can. How old is it? Who did it belong to? And what was it used for?

• If the museum allows you to take photographs, attach them here. If not, visit the gift shop and buy a postcard of your favorite exhibit, to help you remember it.

Whether it's a restored castle, a rare collection of swords, or a small local exhibition, museums can take you on a trip back in time.

In the battlefield

• Arrange a castle visit and be transported into an exciting bygone era. Explore the banqueting hall, castle kitchens, and even dungeons. How many of the castle's defense features can you identify?

• Check the castle's events calendar before you visit. Many castles hold falconry displays or classes to help you perfect your archery skills.

• Visit old churches like Tobias Capwell did in the expert story, looking for medieval effigies of knights depicted in full armor. You may find stained-glass windows with scenes from the Middle Ages. Sketch your finds here.

• Take part in a dig with your local archeologists' club and uncover a knightly artifact yourself.

•Make your own medieval souvenir at a brass rubbing center or castle workshop. These are made by covering a brass with special black paper and rubbing gold or silver wax over the raised engraving until the picture appears.

• See if you can find out the oldest building in your neighborhood. Better still, find out what your area would have looked like in the Middle Ages.

Many magnificent castles are still standing and open to the public. If you can't get to one, there are other ways to bring the medieval world to life.

....

....

....

....

....

....

....

....

....

Research

TOP TIPS

Books
An essential resource for any expert! Visit your local library or bookshop where you can find tales about famous knights, such as King Arthur, or historical information about a specific order of knights that interests you.

The media
Look out for films or TV programs set in medieval times, such as *A Knight's Tale* and *Excalibur!* Watching them may help you get a taste of what the life of a knight may have been like. With your growing knowledge you'll also have fun spotting what's based on fact and what's pure fiction.

The web
There are many websites dedicated to the Middle Ages—some of the best sites are listed on page 68 of your *Eyewitness Knight*. Find a site dedicated to heraldry and genealogy— you may discover that you have a knight in your family tree!

Museums
Go online or check your local newspaper to find out where the nearest exhibition is being held. If you can't get there in person they may have a website where you can take a virtual tour instead.

An expert needs to put in a lot of patient hours of research to trace the history of a castle, artifact, or discover the original wearer of a suit of armor.

....

....

....

....

....

....

....

....

....

Scrapbook

Use this space to attach your sketches, photographs, and postcards. Try drawing the detail of a piece of armor, or an intricate sword!

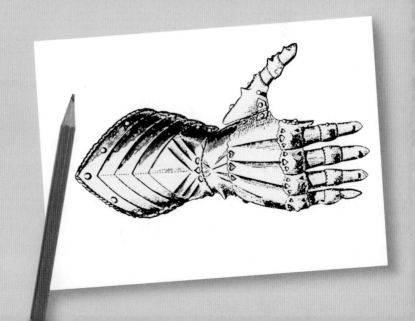

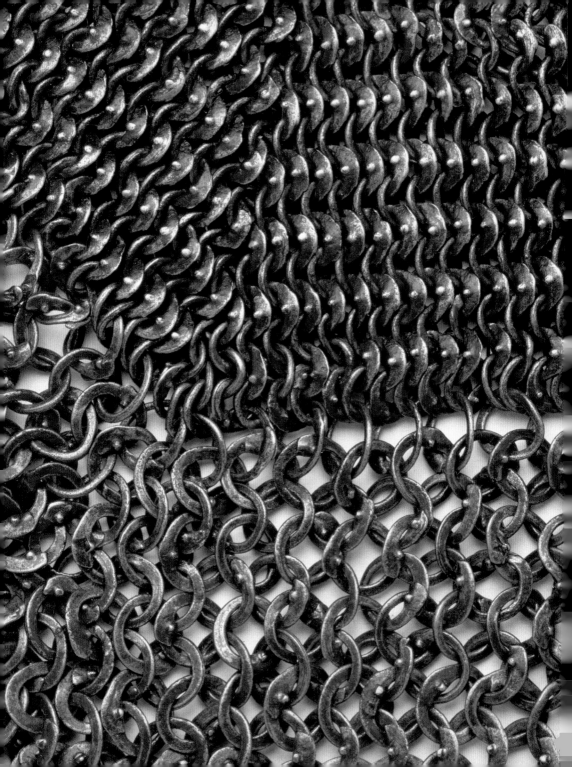

4

PACK MANUAL

Make the most of your interactive pack—discover how experts use maps to plot the past, be inspired to personalize your projects with the clipart CD, and build your own castle by following the step-by-step instructions.

Expert reads

Everything you need to know about getting the most from your interactive expert pack is right here! Written by the experts of today for the experts of tomorrow, these reads will speed you on your journey to discovering the incredible world of knights in the Middle Ages. Read on!

Eyewitness Guide

Your first port of call for all things chivalrous, this museum on a page is where you can be an eyewitness to the everyday life of a medieval warrior. Written by experts and illustrated with close-up photographs of collectors' specimens, *Eyewitness Knight* is an essential read for every budding expert.

Wall chart

How were fortresses built? Who were the first knights? Put this chart on your wall at home or at school and the answers to your knight questions will never be far away.

Arming for the fight

EARLY ARMOR was quite easy to put on. Mail was pulled on over the head, while a coat of plates (pp. 12–13) was buckled at the back, or sides and shoulders. Plate armor was more complicated to put on but a knight could be armed by his squire in a few minutes and the armor could be speedily removed if necessary. After putting on a garment called an arming doublet, a knight was always armed from the feet upward, finishing with the helmet. From the 15th century, some pieces of armor were laced to the arming doublet, but in the following century these pieces were more usually attached to each other by straps or rivets. Here a squire is arming a knight in late 15th-century German "Gothic" style armor.

Mail gusset

Arming doublet

Waxed points

ARMING DOUBLET
This padded garment has
waxed thongs (called points)
sewn to different parts of the
body. Therefore the armor
can be put on without
making the doublet. The mail
covering the doublet cover
which will be left by

Backplate

Flanged edge

**2 SABATON, GREAVE,
POLEYN, AND CUISSE**
The sabaton and greave, for foot and lower leg, are
followed by the poleyn and lower leg, are
cuisse. The top edge is
laced up to the torso.

Breast-plate

Greave

Sabaton

A knight's home

Many knights lived in fortified buildings ca
castles, built around 900, were wooden fortre
mounds. Later, castles were built of stor
battlements, moats, and strong de

Lancet window let in light but kept out missiles

Portcullis (iron gate) could be lowered

Gaps throug which defene could shoot

Mail gusset

Arming doublet

Dov

2

England

PROFILE

Overloo
point t
role i
Nap

E
I

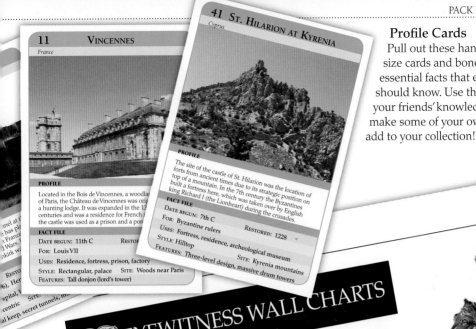

11 VINCENNES

France

PROFILE

Located in the Bois de Vincennes, a woodla[...]
of Paris, the Château de Vincennes was ori[...]
a hunting lodge. It was expanded in the 13[...]
centuries and was a residence for French [...]
the castle was used as a prison and a po[...]

FACT FILE

DATE BEGUN: 11th C   RESTO[...]

FOR: Louis VII

USES: Residence, fortress, prison, factory

STYLE: Rectangular, palace   SITE: Woods near Paris

FEATURES: Tall donjon (lord's tower)

---

41 ST. HILARION AT KYRENIA

Cyprus

PROFILE

The site of the castle of St. Hilarion was the location of
forts from ancient times due to its strategic position on
top of a mountain. In the 7th century the Byzantines
built a fortress here, which was taken over by English
king Richard I (the Lionheart) during the crusades.

FACT FILE

DATE BEGUN: 7th C

FOR: Byzantine rulers   RESTORED: 1228

USES: Fortress, residence, archeological museum

STYLE: Hilltop

FEATURES: Three-level design, massive drum towers   SITE: Kyrenia mountains

---

Profile Cards

Pull out these handy pocket-size cards and bone up on the essential facts that every expert should know. Use them to test your friends' knowledge, too, or make some of your own cards to add to your collection!

DK EYEWITNESS WALL CHARTS

KNIGHT

KNIGHTS WERE WARRIORS WHO FOUGHT ON HORSEBACK. They lived in medieval times in Europe, between c. 1000 and 1500. Knights came from noble families and were trained from boyhood to handle weapons, wear armor, and ride heavy war horses. Some knights owned castles and lands. Others served in the private armies of great lords who, in turn, served the king.

Th[...]

*igh turrets
o watch for
approaching
enemies.*

Moat (ditch filled with water)

*he first
of earthen
owers,*

Mail skirt

Backplate

Waist strap

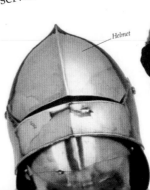

Helmet

Pauldron

Gauntlet

Vambrace

Couter

ARM ARMOR
uter (elbow guard)

6 GA[...]
Ea[...]
with a[...]

Medieval maps

Medieval travelers did not have geographical maps showing accurate locations of parts of the world, but found their way by following the instructions of others who had gone on the journey before. Medieval *mappae mundi*, or world maps, were intended not to help travelers, but to show what many people in the Middle Ages thought the world looked like, based on descriptions in the Bible. Modern historians trying to track past routes have to search for descriptions of where travelers ventured, by examining old paintings, writings, and artifacts. Evidence is also visible in the churches, castles, and markets they set up in places where they stayed.

The Psalter Map
Found in an English Psalter, or book of psalms, dating from about 1262, the Psalter Map is one of the earliest maps to show Jerusalem as the center of the world. The map shows various Biblical events, such as the Flood and crossing the Red Sea, but makes no attempt to be geographically accurate. Historians can tell by comparing maps like these with historical accounts of medieval explorers, including crusaders and traders, that information about routes used was either unknown to, or ignored by, the mapmakers.

Your *Eyewitness* Knight Map

Use your map to travel back to the age of chivalry. Follow crusader and trade routes, and visit some spectacular castles that still inspire awe centuries later. Find out the best sites to build a castle and why.

The Siege of Antioch

Antioch, in Syria, was an important city along the crusaders' route to Jerusalem. This painting shows the crusaders besieging the city. Although it was made much later in the Middle Ages, pictures like this give experts an idea of how crusaders traveled and fought.

Tumbrel
balance

Fair trade

Artifacts help historians to build up a picture of the people who used the trade routes. Merchants in the Middle Ages used portable scales called a tumbrel balance to weigh coins from different regions and work out their value.

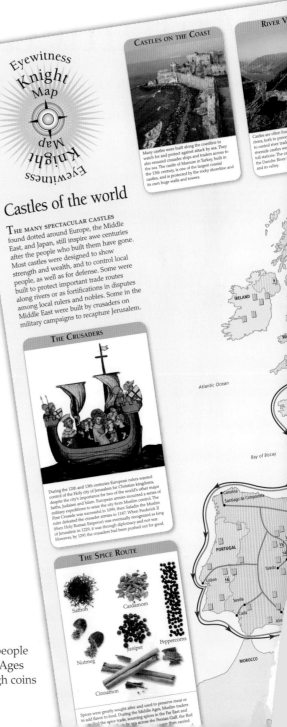

Eyewitness
Knight
Map
ɟɥɓᴉuʞ
Map
ssǝuʇᴉʍǝʎƎ

CASTLES ON THE COAST

Many castles were built along the coastline to watch for and protect against attack by sea. They also ensured crusader ships and traders access to the sea. The castle of Mamure in Turkey, built in the 13th century, is one of the largest coastal castles, and is protected by the rocky shoreline and its own huge walls and towers.

RIVER VIE

Castles are often found rivers, both to preven to control river traffic riverside castles were toll stations. The cas the Danube River in and its valley.

Castles of the world

THE MANY SPECTACULAR CASTLES found dotted around Europe, the Middle East, and Japan, still inspire awe centuries after the people who built them have gone. Most castles were designed to show strength and wealth, and to control local people, as well as for defense. Some were built to protect important trade routes along rivers or as fortifications in disputes among local rulers and nobles. Some in the Middle East were built by crusaders on military campaigns to recapture Jerusalem.

THE CRUSADERS

During the 12th and 13th centuries European rulers wanted control of the Holy city of Jerusalem for Christian kingdoms, despite the city's importance for two of the world's other major faiths, Judaism and Islam. European armies mounted a series of military expeditions to seize the city from Muslim control. The First Crusade was successful in 1099, then Saladin the Muslim ruler defeated the crusader armies in 1187. When Frederick II (then Holy Roman Emperor) was eventually recognized as king of Jerusalem in 1229, it was through diplomacy and not war. However, by 1291 the crusaders had been pushed out for good.

THE SPICE ROUTE

Saffron
Cardamom
Peppercorns
Juniper
Nutmeg
Cinnamon

Spices were greatly sought after and used to preserve meat or to add flavor to food. During the Middle Ages, Muslim traders controlled the spice trade, sourcing spices in the Far East and by sea across the Persian Gulf, the Red then carried

IRELAND

WAL

Atlantic Ocean

Bay of Biscay

Coruña
Santiago de Compostela

PORTUGAL 15
14

Lisbon 16

Toledo

Seville

Cadiz Alm

MOROCCO

Multimedia

History projects have never been so much fun. Packed with 100 specialized images and facts about knights, castles, and medieval life, this clip-art CD will make your homework look so professional, you might even get top grades!

Clip-art CD

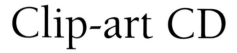

Castles

Crusaders

Swords

For instant pictures, open up your clip-art CD, follow the "how to use" instructions, and explore castles, knights, and medieval life.

Fashions in steel

Your own castle

Build up your knowledge of castle construction by assembling the castle model in your pack. You'll find step-by-step instructions on the next page.

Before you start assembling your castle, press out all the pieces. Open the windows and doors, and push open each slot—you may need a blunt pair of scissors to do this.

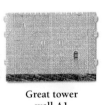

Great tower
wall A1
(outside)

Great tower
inner wall
A2

Middle
floor A4

Top
floor A3

Bottom
A5

Tower
stairs A7

Great tower
outer wall A8
(inside)

Great tower
flat roof A9

Great tower
flat roof A6

Great tower
roof A10

Gatehouse tower B1

Gatehouse tower B2

Main door
frame B3

Middle
frame B4

Portcullis
frame B5

Portcullis
B6

Gatehouse
tower roof B7

Gatehouse
tower roof B8

Outer wall C1 (inside)

Mill tower C2

Mill tower
roof C3

Mural tower C4

Mural tower C5

Outer wall C6

Outer wall C7 (inside)

Chapel
wall C8

Latrine C9

Outer wall C10

Latrine
roof C11

Mural tower
roof C12

Mural tower
roof C13

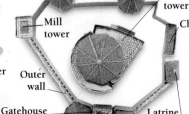

Mural towers

Great
tower

Chapel

Mill
tower

Outer
wall

Gatehouse

Latrine

ASSEMBLING YOUR CASTLE

THE GREAT TOWER

Fold the card along each of the score lines. The numbered tabs are where the pieces slot together.

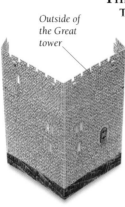

Outside of the Great tower

Bend along each fold so the piece forms a smooth curve.

1 Hold the tower wall A1 with the inside facing you and bend the three folds toward you. The tower will stand up on its own.

2 Take the tower flat roof A6 and insert the tabs into the slots at the top of the tower wall A1. Insert the tabs on the left before those on the right.

3 Hold the inner tower wall A2 with the inside facing you and bend the 14 tabs on tower wall A1 into the slots on inner tower wall A2.

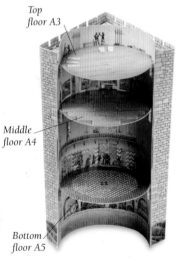

Top floor A3

Middle floor A4

Bottom floor A5

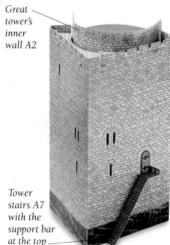

Great tower's inner wall A2

Tower stairs A7 with the support bar at the top

Roll the paper around something narrow and round (such as a rolling pin or broom handle) to help create the curve.

4 Take the top, middle and bottom floors of the Great tower (A3, A4, A5). Make sure the floors, not the ceilings, face upward, and insert the tabs on each piece into the slots on the inner tower wall A2.

5 Hold the tower stairs A7 so the tabs are on the left. Bend the top fold upward to form the support bar. Bend the second fold downward to create the stairs. Now insert the tabs into the slots on the side of the tower wall A1.

6 Take the outer tower wall, piece A8 and making sure that the colorful side of the wall is facing you, curve the piece toward you.

THE GATEHOUSE

Outer tower flat roof A9

Make sure that the flap on the right is inside the cone.

Make sure that the flaps on the right slot inside the tower.

7 Take the outer flat roof A9 and insert the tabs into the slots on the top of the outer tower wall A8. Set this piece aside with the rest of the tower.

8 Hold the tower roof A10 so that the outside is facing you and bend the nine folds to shape the roof. Insert the tab on the left into the slot on the right to form a cone. Put the tower roof and the tower to one side for now.

9 Hold the gatehouse B1 with the inside facing you and bend the folds toward you. To form the tower, place the tabs into the slots. Repeat to make up the second gatehouse tower B2.

Window slits on front side of B1

Slot the tab on the left of the roof into gatehouse tower B1—the tab on the right will slot into gatehouse tower B2.

Gatehouse tower B1

Middle door frame B4

Gatehouse tower B2

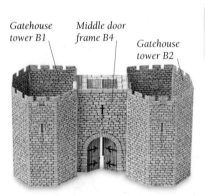

Slide the portcullis B6 into the gap between the portcullis frame B5 and the middle door frame B4.

Front view

10 Hold the main door frame B3 so that the inside is facing you and bend the fold toward you to form a roof. Insert the tabs on the left into the slots on the gatehouse tower B1 and the tabs on the right into gatehouse tower B2 to join the towers together.

11 Take the middle door frame B4 and insert the two tabs on each side into the slots toward the front of gatehouse towers B1 and B2.

12 Hold the portcullis frame B5 so that the inside is facing you. Bend the top fold toward you and the bottom fold away from you to form the battlements. Place the two tabs on either side into the slots at the very front of gatehouse towers B1 and B2. There will be a gap between the two frames.

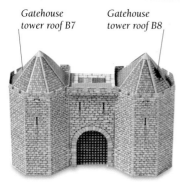

Gatehouse tower roof B7

Gatehouse tower roof B8

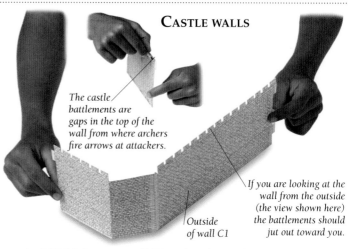

CASTLE WALLS

The castle battlements are gaps in the top of the wall from where archers fire arrows at attackers.

Outside of wall C1

If you are looking at the wall from the outside (the view shown here) the battlements should jut out toward you.

13 Construct both gatehouse tower roofs following the instructions given for step 8. Ensure that the flap on the right is inside the cone. Fold the tabs at the base of the cone B7 at right angles and slide them into the slots in the gatehouse tower B1. Repeat to make gatehouse tower roof B8 and slot that into B2.

14 Hold the outer wall C1 so that the inside is facing you and bend the two vertical folds toward you, so that the wall stands up. Then push out the battlements by bending the first fold away from you and the second fold (with the crenallations) toward you.

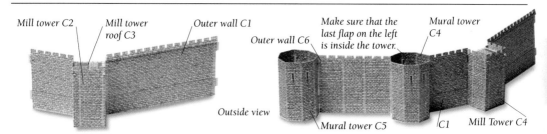

Mill tower C2

Mill tower roof C3

Outer wall C1

Outside view

Outer wall C6

Make sure that the last flap on the left is inside the tower.

Mural tower C4

Mural tower C5

C1

Mill Tower C4

15 Hold the Mill tower C2 so that the outside is facing you and bend the two folds away from you. Insert the two tabs into the slots on the two folds of the outer wall C1. Take the Mill tower roof C3. Insert two tabs into the slots on Mill tower C2.

16 With the inside of the Mural tower C4 facing you, bend the folds toward you. Insert the tabs into the slots to form a tower. Repeat to make up the second mural tower C5. Insert the tabs on the left of outer wall C1 into the slots of mural tower C4. Take the outer wall C6 and insert the tabs into the slots on mural tower C4 and mural tower C5.

Outer wall C7

Mill tower C2

Mural tower C4

Mural tower C5

Outer wall C6

17 Hold the outer wall C7 so that the outside is facing you. Starting from the left, bend the first and second folds away from you, the third and fourth folds toward you and the fifth fold away from you. Insert the tabs on the right-hand side into the slots on mural tower C5.

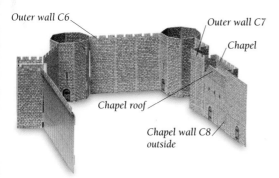

Outer wall C6
Outer wall C7
Chapel
Chapel roof
Chapel wall C8
outside

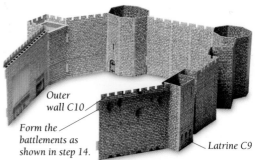

Outer
wall C10
Form the
battlements as
shown in step 14.
Latrine C9

18 Hold the chapel wall C8 so that the inside is facing you. Bend the two horizontal folds toward you to form a pointed chapel roof. Insert the two tabs (87 and 88) into the slots in the center of the outer wall C7. (The two decorated chapel walls will be inside.) Then push the tabs on the right of C7 into the center slots on chapel wall C8.

19 Hold the latrine C9 so that the outside is facing you and bend the two folds away from you. Insert the four tabs into the slots on the chapel wall C8. Hold the outer wall C10 so that the outside is facing you and push out the battlements as before. Insert the tabs on the right into the slots on the latrine C9.

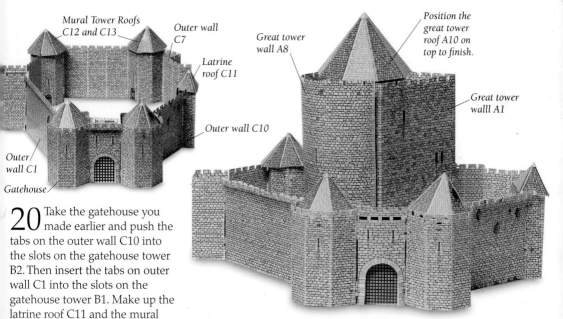

Mural Tower Roofs
C12 and C13
Outer wall
C7
Great tower
wall A8
Position the
great tower
roof A10 on
top to finish.
Latrine
roof C11
Great tower
walll A1
Outer wall C10
Outer
wall C1
Gatehouse

20 Take the gatehouse you made earlier and push the tabs on the outer wall C10 into the slots on the gatehouse tower B2. Then insert the tabs on outer wall C1 into the slots on the gatehouse tower B1. Make up the latrine roof C11 and the mural tower roofs C12 and C13 (as before in step 8). Place the roofs on top of the towers.

21 To finish off the castle, take the Great tower made in steps 1-7 and place it inside the outer wall as shown in the photograph. When positioning the great tower, slide the two halves of the tower (outer tower wall A8 and tower wall A1) together so that inside of the great tower is enclosed, then put the roof on top.

Index

Activity answers

Page 30–31 A knight's world
1. C 800
2. D 1066
3. F 1100s
4. E 1118
5. B 1346
6. A 1517

Spot the castle
A. Caerlaverock, Scotland
B. Caernarfon, Wales
C. Krak des Chevaliers, Syria
D. Saumur, France
E. Akershus, Norway
F. Coca, Spain

Page 32–33 Know your armor
1. Bellows visor
2. Gorget plates
3. Pauldron
4. Besagew
5. Lance rest
6. Breastplate
7. Couter
8. Vambrace
9. Mitten gauntlet
10. Cuisse
11. Poleyn
12. Wing on poleyn
13. Greave
14. Sabaton

Helmets
a. France, 16th century
b. Italy, 14th century
c. Germany, 15th century
d. Germany 16th century
e. Italy, 16th century
f. Italy, 15th century

Page 34–35 Dressing a knight
A. 2 Cuisse
B. 5 Couter
C. 7 Helmet
D. 6 Gauntlet
E. 4 Back plate
F. 1 Arming doublet
G. 3 Mail skirt

Sword search
1 Two-hand sword
2. Pole ax
3. Sword with
   copper-gilt guard
4. Mace
5. Dagger

Name this item
Shaffron
To protect the top of a horse's head

Page 36–37 Showy shields
a. Gules, lion rampant or
b. Or, a portcullis purpure
c. Azure, a Sun in splendor or
d. Sable, a cross engrailed or
e. Or, a dragon rampant vert
f. Vert, a castle argent

Joust a minute
1 Reins
2 Trapper
3 Mail
4 Helmet
5 Lance
6 Saddle
7 Stirrup

Page 38–39 Castle as kingdom

Great Hall · Lord's apartment · Battlement · Gatehouse · Drawbridge · Moat · Slit window · Mural tower · Kitchen garden · Storerooms

Page 38–39 Castle shields
 Shape sorter
1. Motte & bailey
2. Keep
3. Concentric

Defense and attack
Trebuchet — Both
Battering ram — Attack
Embrasure — Defense
Crossbow — Both
Portcullis — Defense

Acknowledgments

The publisher would like to thank the following for their kind permission to reproduce their photographs:

(Key: a–above; b–below/bottom; c–center; f–far; l–left; r–right; t–top)

Expert Files
akg-images: 25bl; **Alamy Images:** Paul Felix Photography 19tr; **Albion Swords Ltd.:** Lutz Hoffmeister 17tr; **American Museum Of Natural History:** 23c; **The Board of Trustees of the Armories:** 10t; **Courtesy of Bamburgh Castle:** 19b; **British Library:** 54; **Courtesy of Dominique Buttin:** 22tr; **Corbis:** The Art Archive 55tl; Ronald Wittek/dpa 18r; Martyn Goddard 6-7; Gianni Dagli Orti 22b; **Geoff Dann** 5b; **DK Images:** By kind permission of the trustees of the Trustees of The Wallace Collection 32cl, 32-33b, 33tr, 56bl, 56br, 56cl, 56crb, 56fbl, 56fbr; **English Arms & Armor:** David Laity 20l, 20r; **Mark Coutts Photography:** 1,

8-9b, 11r, 11tl, 15r; **Middelaldercentret, Denmark:** 29cra; **National Portrait Gallery,** London: 25c; **The National Trust Photo Library:** Ian Shaw 18tl; **Oxford Film and Television:** 24tr; **Laurence Pordes** Courtesy of The British Library 29br; **SAS VR/Steve Shearn:** 19c; **TopFoto.co.uk:** Silvio Fiore 23br; **By kind permission of the trustees of the Wallace Collection,** London: 16, 29br.

Map
Corbis/Bettmann br; **DK Images:** Paul Whitfield/ Rough Guides trc; Oesterreich Werbung (Austrian National Tourist Office) tlc; The Art Archive/ Bibliothèque Nationale Paris / JFB cl.

Profiles
See Page 16 of *Knight Profiles*

Wall chart
See Page 72 of *Eyewitness Knight*

Clip-art CD
See the *Credits* file on the CD

All other images © Dorling Kindersley
For further information see: **www.dkimages.com**

The publisher would also like to thank:
Boundford.com for cartography on the Map;
Stewart Wild for proofreading;
Hilary Bird for the index;
Margaret Parrish for Americanization.

Professor Anne Curry's database of soldiers is at:
www.medievalsoldier.org.